HOW TO BE A GOOD FRIEND

Information and Encouragement with Inspirational Short Stories by Teens and Young Adults

Jennifer Leigh Youngs, A.A. · Bettie B. Youngs, Ph.D., Ed.D.

from the SMART TEENS-SMART CHOICES series

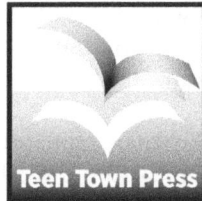

Teen Town Press
www.TeenTownPress.com

an imprint of Bettie Youngs Book Publishers, Inc.

Cover Graphic Design: Adrian Pitariu and Beau Kimbrel
Text Design: Beau Kimbrel
Teen Consultant: Kendahl Brooke Youngs

TEEN TOWN PRESS / www.TeenTownPress.com is an Imprint of Bettie Youngs Book Publishing Co., Inc.:
www.BettieYoungsBooks.com.

If you are unable to order this book from your local bookseller or online, or Ingram Book Group, order directly from the publisher:
info@BettieYoungsBooks.com.

PRINT ISBN: 978-1-940784-73-1
DIGITAL ISBN: 978-1-940784-72-4

10 9 8 7 6 5 4 3 2

Library of Congress Cataloging-in-Publication Data Available upon Request.

Summary: Information and encouragement with inspirational short stories by teens and young adults discussing making and keeping friends, and mending hurt feelings. 1. YAN literature. 2. Friends. 3. Virtues. 4. Teens and Young Adults. 5. Relationships. 6. Friendships. 7. Values. 8. Confidence. 9. Peer Pressure. 10. Youngs, Bettie B. 11. Youngs, Jennifer Leigh. 12. Youngs, Kendahl Brooke.

Also by the Authors for Teens and Young Adults

How Your Brain Decides If You Will Become Addicted—Or Not

Setting and Achieving Goals that Matter TO ME

Managing the Stress, Pressure and the Ups and Downs of Life

The 10 Commandments and the Secret Each One Guards—FOR YOU

How to Be Courageous

Growing Your Confidence and Self-Esteem

Faith at Work in Our Lives

Understanding Feelings of Love

How to Have a Great Attitude

Understanding the Christian Faith

How to be a Good Friend

The Power of Being Kind, Courteous and Thoughtful

Caring for Your Body's Health and Wellness

Having Healthy and Beautiful Hair, Skin and Nails

Inspirational Stories and Encouragement on Friends and the Face in the Mirror

CONTENTS

3. MY PERSONAL WORKBOOK: HOW TO BE A GOOD FRIEND
- Being a Friend to Yourself Begins with Liking YOU
- Helping Other Get to Know You—the "Real" You
- Standing Up For Yourself
- Expressing Yourself Clearly
- What is a "Friend"?
- Breakups, and Makeups
- Working Through Disagreements
- Who Are Your "Real" Friends?
- Showing Acceptance of Self, and Others
- What are the "Rules" for Being YOUR Friend?
- Making Friends
- Treating Friends Right
- Ending Friendships

OTHER BOOKS BY THE AUTHORS

CHAPTER 1

FRIENDSHIP: A NECESSITY OF LIFE

When an elephant is ill or injured, other elephants in the herd gather around to protect the animal, and to bolster it up. They know how important their support is because if an elephant in such a condition lays down, it won't be able to stand up again on its own. So, the other members of the herd literally surround the weak elephant and help it remain standing. Even when on the move, the other elephants walk next to the ailing elephant, supporting it as they travel.

Just as elephants intuitively know when one of their friends needs their support, they also know when to back away.

Amazing, isn't it, that elephants intuitively know when one of their friends needs their help! Friendships are like that.

Friends: Pizza For Life!

A good friend is someone we can count on and with whom we can have fun with, and share our innermost thoughts, secrets, lofty and noble goals, and our hopes, joys and fears. A good friend allows us a safe space to share our thoughts without worry of being judged for feeling the way we do. Friends cheer each other on, laugh and cry and listen to each other. That's *why* friends are *friends*.

A good friend helps you become a better, wiser and more compassionate person than you might have been without that friend in your life. Friends help us grow into being who we are or, as Jennifer Leigh said, "A friend is someone with whom I can reveal the many sides of me, some I am meeting for the first time, myself!"

What a wonderful gift.

As you'll see from the stories by young people you'll meet in this book, young people value their friends, and the important role their friends play in their lives in coping with the everyday ups and downs of life. Seventeen-year-old Roma Kipling's friends gathered around when she lost her beloved grandmother, as did a friend of fifteen-year-old Curt Lindholm when he lost a brother. For both Roma and Curt, it was a friend—and the love and support from their families—who "held their heart" through a sorrow-filled experience that was so meaningful to each.

Friends: Help Shape Our "Sense of Self"

Each of us longs to "be ourselves." And yet, we seek the approval of others. We often think:

"Do you think I'm okay?"

"Do you accept me as I am?"
"Do you like the way I look?"
"Do you approve of how I act?"
"Do you like me?"
"Will you be my friend?"

We want the answers to each of these questions to be a wholehearted, "Yes!"

When others like us and accept us, we feel worthy—like we're a terrific person. But even though we may want to feel liked and accepted by others, we may not always get a positive response; some people may not think as much of us as we would like. Sometimes this doesn't bother us, but most of the time, especially if their approval is important to us, it's only natural to feel rejected, hurt or left out.

All of us are vulnerable to the scrutiny of others. Why are we so sensitive to their review of us? We want them to accept and approve of who we are at our inner level, not just for what they see of us at the surface. What we really want is for others to like and accept us for who we are—as we are. But what if they don't like what they see? The fear of being rejected is at the heart of the struggle between hiding and revealing our true selves and can cause us to feel as though even the people closest to us don't really understand us all that well.

Many young people feel that in order to win favor and friendship from others, they must "play into" or portray an image they believe someone else holds of them, rather than "be themselves." It's a "coat of paint" that no one likes to be burdened by wearing. The price-tag for being "someone else" comes at a loss of true identity. Sometimes the loss includes self-respect and self-esteem. The good news is, while you are willing to do some things to gain acceptance, there's a limit. Feeling uneasy about covering up who you are in order to be liked by someone else is a healthy feeling. You are you—and that is who you are supposed to be. You shouldn't have to become someone you're not.

Perhaps that's what made "The Paintbrush" (found in the workbook section of this book) such a popular piece with so many! Said Brianna Stavros, "The poem, The Paintbrush, really describes my feelings because it's hard to stay true to yourself, yet be liked and considered worthy without having to "cover up other parts of you."

Friends: Begin with Being a Happy Person

Being happy with yourself is the starting point for being a successful human being and to best experience success in the world around you. But as the old saying goes, "No man is an island." We live in a world with others, and just about everything we do is done in concert with them. We live in families and within communities; we go to school and work with others. We communicate with people on a daily basis. As we learn the best ways to live in tandem with others, we find that moving from "me" to "you" adds yet another dimension to our inner contentment. Being on friendly terms with others is a good feeling and important.

Imagine what it's like going to school in the morning and not having anyone save you a place on the bus, or in the cafeteria or at the assembly. Imagine not having a friend to hang out with when you want to "check out" the guys or girls! A big part of the experience of being a young person is doing things for the first time and learning to do things in your own way. It just wouldn't be fun, much less comfortable, to do those things all alone. Having someone you like, a good friend, makes the experience more fun.

Friends are a huge part of what makes your young adult years fun, and is confirmation, validation, and a baseline by which to gauge how you are doing and faring.

Friendships: Teach Us About Ourselves

Acceptance and belonging are powerful feelings within our hearts—necessities that, for better or for worse, shape our lives.

As we learn and grow, we discover that life with others is not just about how to navigate the waters of getting along with a wide array of personalities. Friendships are also about lessons, teaching us so much about ourselves—as expressed in the beautiful and eloquent words of Anaïs Nin: *"Each friend represents a world in us, a world possibly not born until they arrive."*

People enter our lives and change it in some way: each new friend represents a new possibility to see ourselves and our lives in a whole new way.

That a special friend can open our eyes to a new idea, changing the way we see the world and ourselves, is one of the reasons we guard our friendships and treat each friend as special.

As so many of us find out, friends can be the very best mirrors we have. Not only are they willing to honestly assess how we're looking, they also view us with hopeful eyes. Never is this a greater gift than when we're being hard on ourselves. A friend offers understanding and acceptance during times when we struggle to understand and accept ourselves. In a world that can seem overwhelming, friends offer us the comfort of connection: with friends we're not in it alone! Friends make the whole world seem like a kinder place.

Good friends can help us grow into the sort of person we wish to be, to put our best foot forward, to strive toward goals that may seem too lofty to tell others for fear they will not support us in going toward our dream.

Friends: Are Good Listeners

As much as friends are friends, they still have to pass the standards you set for friendship, such as being able to talk openly and honestly about things, or as Elmer Adrian said, "if you can't talk openly, our story ends."

Many young people said that they expected their friends to acknowledge them when they did something especially good—like aced an exam, or played well in a tournament or, looked extra cool. That a friend is able to give you feedback about these things is more than just a matter of praise; it encourages and inspires you to continue to do and be your best.

Being able to express yourself is important between friends—as an entire auditorium of teens found out during a school assembly when Rob Ballen, seventeen, the good-looking, three-time-elected student-council president took the stage. His classmates described Rob as "a scholar and a gentleman," "every girl's dream boat," and "every guy's idol." His classmates were in awe of him. You can imagine how surprised they were when they learned Rob was not as happy as they thought he was. Rob talked about how he thought of himself as shy, was nervous about speaking in front of his class, and told of ways he often felt unsure of himself, even insecure.

Good communication is not always easy, as Belinda Carr, sixteen, points out, but it has its benefits—as sixteen-year-old Beth Brown discovered: "Being allowed to spend time with my friends means knowing how to communicate effectively with my parents." But, an often overlooked fact of being a good communicator is that it is primarily based on being a good listener.

If you watch closely, you'll notice that the best-liked and most popular people spend as much time listening to others as they do talking. Being a good listener is also one of the most important aspects of making and keeping friends, and of getting along with others.

Do you know someone who pretends to listen, but continually interrupts, acts bored or shows indifference to what you're saying? It doesn't feel good to have someone do this to you. In fact, it makes you feel unimportant, and makes it pretty clear that you have nothing interesting to say. A teacher did an experiment that pointed out how unnerving this is. It was a day when students were to give an oral report in front of the class. Trent—a really popular and well-liked student— was called to the counselor's office in the middle of his presentation.

This was a set-up, but Trent didn't know it. When he left the room, the teacher instructed other students in the class, that when Trent returned they were to be "an obnoxious audience." Some were to lay their heads down on others desk, others were to gaze out the window and still others were to pretend to scowl or shake their heads in disagreement.

When Trent returned to the classroom and continued his presentation, the class went into their "awful listeners" mode. After only a few minutes of speaking, a very frustrated Trent stopped and asked, "What is going on? Why are you treating me this way?"

Listening is an attitude. If you want others to by your friend, you must want to listen and not just wait for your turn to talk. Look at that person, show your interest, suspend all judgment and just listen. Let the person who is speaking finish before you say anything. This shows that you care enough to listen and that you respect the person enough to care about what he or she has to say. It also gives you time to think about what the person is saying and an opportunity to gather your thoughts and decide how to respond.

Try it and you'll be amazed at how much it improves your friendships and increases your popularity with others.

Friends: Are Kind and Considerate

Another good communication skill in creating and keeping friends is being kind and treating others as you would want to be treated. Being kind shows that you are a happy person who likes herself and that you are considerate and thoughtful. And, it helps confirm that friends are "real friends," as sixteen-year-old poet Peggy Nunziata tells us in her poem (found in Chapter Two).

Accepted by others, and to feel as if we belong, supports our natural instincts for self-acceptance making us feel whole and sure of ourselves.

Belonging is a powerful contribution to how secure, happy and content we are within our own lives.

In the next chapter, you'll read stories by your "peers" talking about "friends"—making, keeping, and sometimes, leaving them behind as well as ways some friends become friends for life.

Enjoy their stories!

A word from the authors: While friends are there for us when we walk through heartache and grief, sometimes we need even more support. Should you be going through a difficult time, we urge you to seek the support of your family, as well as a teacher, school counselor or pastor—to help you get the support you need.

CHAPTER 2

STORIES ABOUT THE IMPORTANCE OF FRIENDSHIP—BY TEENS AND YOUNG ADULTS

The Way It Is

Friends . . .

Laughing
Talking
Sharing

Blaming
Shouting
Crying

Explaining
Apologizing
Giggling

Laughing
Talking
Sharing

Blaming

Shouting
Crying

Explaining
Apologizing
Giggling

Laughing
Talking
Sharing

Friends. It's just the way it is.
                    —Jeanna Renee Withers, 14

You Are an Inspiring Friend

Sometimes I wonder
What it's like to be you,
To bring so much joy
The way that you do.

To make people smile
Day after day,
To speak words of wisdom
Others trust what you say.

When someone's upset
In a funk, or a pout,
You soothe and you comfort
They no longer worry or doubt.

You're a great personality
You have your own style,
It's real and it's genuine—
What an awesome profile.

You never give up
You always succeed,
You do not follow
You have your own lead.

It's amazing to think
How many lives you've touched—
And mine is one of them!
Thank you so much!

You're a great inspiration
And a person who's kind,
A friend like you
Is a really good find!

—**Ashley Kuiken, 14**

Our Friendship Is Real

I'm sitting here thinking about the past,
Hoping in the future our friendship will last.
We have been friends for a short time,
Been through a lot, and doing just fine.

I've seen lots of people come and go,
Saying and doing whatever—careless, you know?
That's why your friendship means so much to me,
When I'm with you, I feel secure, whole, and
"me."

I'll be your friend, too, I'll be around,
When times get tough, and we're in a frown.
You'll be there and understand how I feel,
Because we both know our friendship is real.

—**Peggy Nunziata, 16**

For You to Cry In

My grandmother was one of my very favorite
people in all the world. Her name was Tilly, but
I called her "Grams." She liked that. Grams was
so much fun to be around. She lived in a small
apartment about forty-five minutes away from my
family. She visited us often, and we visited her quite
a bit, too. She lived her life to the fullest, and was
always very involved in each one of ours. Just this
past summer, she took me with her on vacation, a
vacation she planned with just the two of us in mind.
"Just us two girls," grams told everyone. We went
to Washington, D.C., for eight days. While we were
there, we went to the White House and the Lincoln
Memorial. We visited museums Grams said I had to
know about, and other "places of interest." And we
got to eat dinner in a restaurant every single night.
It was so much fun!

Grams had a way of making everything exciting.
One night we went to a theater to see an opera.
Everyone was dressed up, really dressed up, like in
tuxedos and long gowns. Grams and I dressed up,
too. We even had our hair styled at a salon. In my
opinion, the opera itself wasn't all that great, but
being with Grams sure was. And she was right when
she said it was fun to "appreciate the ambience."
Everybody at the opera was so cool!

Besides being fun to be around, Grams was one
of the most positive people I've known. She had
a way of making me feel like I was truly special.

She believed in me and felt I could do anything I wanted, and that I would. She told everyone that I was "destined to grow up and change the world." She'd tell everyone she introduced me to, "My granddaughter is going to become a very important person, you just watch and see. Someday she'll be president of the United States, or maybe she'll just create the cure for all diseases—or the formula to make everyone in the world happy and forever young!"

She was like that. With her, I was an "unlimited" person.

But then, when she was only sixty-one years old, Grams died. I had visited her only two days before. She seemed healthy and was her usual, happy self. Mom said she died from a brain aneurysm.

When it happened, I was heartsick.

Knowing how much I loved and missed my grandmother, my two best friends rallied around me. Their parents allowed them to stay home from school and go with me to my grandmother's funeral, a gesture I hadn't expected. And the days following my grandmother's death they were so extra kind and sensitive to my feelings. Regularly they asked, "Are you doing okay?" or "Are you feeling better?" I found that so loving, and it showed me that they understood the hurt I was feeling.

The evening after the funeral, both of them came to my house. They brought me a stuffed animal with a note: *"For you to cry in."* They both stayed over that night, which was really nice. We just hung out, doing things like rearranging my closet, listening to music and talking.

My friends' empathy toward my sadness was like a big comforting pillow. They really cared and understood. It was so consoling, and it gave me a sense of friendship that I hadn't really felt from friends before. It helped ease the pain I felt over Grams's death.

Since that time, our friendship has been solid, and we're tighter than ever. We help each other through the tough times and we help each other with the important things—like getting dressed to go out on a big date (a team effort), and planning what to wear to school when something big is going on and we want to look extra-great. We trade clothes, fashion and makeup tips or model a potential outfit and exchange brutally honest opinions about what looks best and where and why something doesn't work. Because we are such good friends, we can do this without misunderstandings and hurt feelings.

I will always miss Grams. She was such a good friend; it showed in everything she did. I think it's possible to take friends for granted, and to think that friends are friends no matter what—which is not necessarily so. It doesn't just happen. More than anyone else, it was Grams's "style" of friendship that helps me understand that a friendship is special because of the things that people do to make it special.

The relationship between my grandmother and me was special because Grams made a point of making it special—like my friends and I do for each other.

—Roma Kipling, 17

A Bad Day for the Rest of the Day

When I'm in an argument with my mom or dad, I have a bad day for the rest of the day. It's not like I can have an argument with my parents and then go to school and just forget about it. It's very upsetting. If my parents and I have had an argument, I can be sitting in class, but I'm not really paying attention to what's going on because I'm off in my mind, still thinking about the argument. Rather than concentrating on what the teacher is saying, I'm still involved: What were my parents thinking? Why did they say what they did (or didn't)? Then I wonder why I said what I did—or why I didn't say what I should have! And then I try to decide on a good time and a good way to reopen a conversation with them so I can go where I wanted or get what I wanted, or have what I wanted in the first place!

So I sit in class, planning a new strategy, and playing through every possible response—several times. Which means, of course, that I'm still not paying attention to what's going on in my class. This upsets me too, so then I get worked up all over again.

I'm sure I'm not the only one this happens to. My friends feel equally upset when they aren't on good terms with their parents. So, even though it's really important to me to feel close to my friends, it means even more to me to feel close to my parents.

When my parents and I are seeing eye-to-eye, a lot of things in my life look okay to me.

—Megan Burns, 16

My Stand-In Brother

One day when I was in the eighth grade, my grandfather came to school to get me. This was in the middle of the day, so I knew something was wrong.

We drove to the hospital, and it wasn't until we were getting out of the car that he told me that my brother, Tim, had collapsed on the school playground during recess. They had rushed Tim to the hospital, where he lay in a coma. He was only seven years old.

When I saw my brother hooked up to the wires and tubes, I felt sick to my stomach. It was scary. There were all sorts of monitors on, and he had wires attached to his arms and legs, and tubes in his mouth and nose. I didn't know what all the tubes were supposed to do, but I did know Timmy needed them to stay alive. I wanted to touch Timmy to let him know that I was there, but I didn't because I thought one of the wires or tubes might come unhooked and he'd die because of it. I was worried that Timmy might be in a lot of pain, only we wouldn't know it because he was in a coma and couldn't tell us. I felt so helpless.

The doctors advised my parents to stay at the hospital with Timmy as much as they could. Sometimes they took turns staying, but mostly both stayed. Because I had to go to school each day, my mother called the parents of my friend, Stephen, and asked if I could stay with their family until Timmy got better and my parents didn't have to stay there every night. Stephen's parents said I could stay as long as was needed.

Stephen's parents were really good to me. They made sure I got my homework done, but they also let me watch television a little later than my normal bedtime. And each day right after school, Stephen's mother took me to the hospital to see my brother. Stephen came along.

Seeing my brother in the hospital bed covered in all those wires and tubes never got easier. And I never got over feeling that the tubes might come unhooked if I touched him, so I wouldn't go into Timmy's room unless someone was with me. Seeing Timmy so lifeless was just a very sad feeling. And even when I just sat there, talking with Timmy, hoping he'd wake up and say something, I felt sad being in the room. Not only was it sad to see my brother that way, but my parents were so upset over Timmy's condition, that it hurt to look at them. They tried to be brave and positive, but I could see how fearful they were. I knew that wasn't a good sign; even though they said Timmy was getting better, I didn't believe them. It got to a point where I didn't want to go to the hospital unless Stephen went with me.

Seeing my brother must have been as frightening to Stephen as it was to me, but he always went with me anyway. He never complained about going, either.

One night at Stephen's house, I was sleeping on the floor of his room in a sleeping bag. All the nights while my brother was in the hospital, I didn't sleep very well, but this one night was the worst. I was crying and it woke up Stephen. He asked me if he should get his parents. I thought that showed understanding. He didn't just go and get his parents, he asked if that's what I wanted.

I told him that I didn't need his parents, that it was just that I had a nightmare that Timmy had died. When I told Stephen more about the nightmare, he didn't think I was weird. He just listened. And even though I started crying, he didn't tell me not to.

Stephen said, "It's gotta be really hard to think of losing your own brother." And so we started talking about dying and what that must be like. My parents never talked with me about dying. They didn't want to think that it might really happen. It helped that I could be honest about everything I was feeling.

"The thought of Timmy dying scares me," I told Stephen. "He's just a little kid. And he's the only brother I have." Stephen nodded and then he said, "I hope Timmy doesn't die. But if he does, and you ever need a brother, I'll be your stand-in brother."

My parents called very early the next morning for me to come to the hospital. When I got there, they told me that my brother had died.

I miss my brother every day. We shared a room and sometimes we shared things like our video games and jokes and what we thought about school or different people. Timmy was a good-natured and funny guy, and a very good friend.

Now, on those times when I miss Timmy the most, or just need to remember Timmy by talking about him, I know who to call: Stephen, my stand-in brother. He's always there for me to talk to. And many times, just to listen.

—**Curt Lindholm, 15**

Broken Pact

Nick and Peter were my two best buddies. We always had so much fun together.

Six months ago on a Saturday evening, we went to a friend's house for a party.

Our friend Peter, drank a whole lot of beer; were having fun and didn't stop him.

That wasn't our biggest mistake that evening: we violated our friendship rule.

The three of us had a pact between us that we always looked out for each other. We always made sure that all three of us left together. If we got separated, the plan was always to meet back at the car.

But on this night, we didn't look out for each other as usual: The police raided the party, and we each hightailed it out of there.

Instead of meeting at the car like we planned, Peter didn't show up. We just figured that maybe he had left with a friend or, maybe he had gotten arrested.

As it turned out, in trying to get away from the party Peter had gone down to the beach.

They found Peter the next day, drowned.

I still can't believe that my friend is dead.

It's taken us all a long time to get over Peter's death. Actually, we still aren't over it, and I doubt we ever will be. I know for sure that we'll never get over letting him down. We let each other down.

I know now the importance of the responsibility you have in being a good friend. I know my sorrow will be with me a very long time to come.

—**Lamont Henry, 17**

Most Valuable Player

I've discovered that being around someone who believes you're a terrific person, makes you feel that you are a terrific person. And because of that, you automatically want that person for a friend.

The person who sees and brings out the best in me is Chad Diamant. People say that Chad is a "really together guy," and I can see why: He feels really secure within himself and makes others feel more confident, too. Chad has a special knack for seeing the "up" side of life.

To him, the glass is never half-empty. It's always half-full. A good example is when I play in a football game. If I do well, he has no problem congratulating me on a good game and making me feel like a hero. And if I have a really bad game, in which I play really poorly, he doesn't focus on that. Instead, he points out some of the good aspects of my playing, like how I helped team member to score or make a good play. He turns it around so that once again I end up looking like the most valuable player.

Even if our team lost, he won't dwell on the loss. Instead, he'll talk about some aspect of the game or particular plays that were especially good. "Lousy game," I'll say.

"No way!" he'll counter, and then say something like, "You were great in the third quarter!"

With Chad I can't lose: I'm an MVP every game.

Because of Chad's support and positive attitude, he's the first guy I look for when I come out of the locker room. I consider him the most valuable friend I have, a real MVP in the game of life.

I hope we will be friends for life.

—**Bradley Dawson, 17**

I Keep My Earplugs Handy

Sometimes you don't think about your parents as being friends, but they can be. Mine are.

My dream is to be a professional musician. I'd like to be a real star. Sometimes when I tell that to some of my school friends, especially those who don't know me all that well, they look at me and give a little laugh, like they don't know how to take it. You know . . . am I a serious talent or am I an egotistical jerk? My parents don't laugh or question me. And they didn't doubt that I could learn to play a saxophone. They bought me one last year.

I didn't realize a saxophone was so hard to learn!

I know I must have made a lot of racket as I tried to play it, but my mom and dad never complained.

"Sounds great!" Dad tells me.

"You're really getting good!" Mom says.

Four months ago, I had just about decided it was too much for me to master, but both Mom and Dad assured me that they had no doubts I could do it. So I didn't give up. Like my Dad says, "You can do anything you set your mind on." I love how my parents support me; I really honor that.

So, when I do make it as a professional, I'll owe a lot of my success to my parents for buying me my saxophone of course, but also for believing in me. Until then, I just picture myself up there on stage with the bright lights. And in the front row I see my two best friends—my mom and dad—with their little black shades on, clapping their hands, smiling.

Oh yeah! I'll make them proud!

I just need to keep practicing. And my earplugs handy!

—**Jeremiah White, 17**

Did I Pass Your Test For Friends?

I try to read your eyes,
surmise,
just what you think
behind that brow.
As you nod,
are you thinking
that I am odd?

You seem not to be impressed
at what you see;
I am
a nonentity?
You're in a hurry to forget,
What made me second-class?
I see I didn't pass
the standards you have set
for friends.

Our story ends.

—Elmer Adrian, 93

The Secret She Kept

For almost the entire school year, I liked a boy named Ben. I was pretty sure he didn't know. I never told him. Besides my mom, the only other person who knew was MaryAnn Drew, and I'd sworn her to secrecy! I didn't tell anyone else because it might get back to Ben. What if he didn't feel the same way? I was too shy to take the chance he might feel differently than I did.

"Asking Ben to the Sadie Hawkins dance?" Mom asked.

"I'd love to; I just don't have the nerve," I told her.

"Hmmm," she said, and then told me a story about "two very close friends" of hers when she was in school. Her story goes like this:

Katie liked a boy named Sean. But she never told him, forever keeping the secret to herself. When she saw him sitting at the other end of the lunch table, or with friends, she couldn't help but admire the way he listened intently to his friends, and always seemed so considerate.

Eventually both Sean and Katie began to date—but not each other. On so many occasions, Katie secretly wished her date was Sean, rather than who she was with—but it was her date, and not Sean, who asked her out. The night of her senior prom was especially bittersweet. When a favorite song of hers by Anne Murray was played (a song that always made her think about Sean), she looked to Sean, dancing with his date. Sean was looking in Katie's direction. They smiled at each other, their smiles lingering.

For the entire evening, Katie gazed at Sean dancing with his girlfriend, Annie Pauls. Annie was so outgoing, Katie just knew she'd never stand a chance, even if she did get up the nerve to talk to Sean. But that didn't keep her from looking and dreaming—and wishing it was her dancing in Sean's arms.

After graduating from high school, both Katie and Sean went away to college in different states. But Katie never stopped thinking about Sean.

Years later, both Katie and Sean attended their five-year high school reunion. When the band began to play, both Katie and Sean found themselves standing alone, each looking for a dance partner. Many of their classmates were married and were there with their spouses—but neither Katie nor Sean had married.

Katie looked at Sean across the room, and though butterflies took flight in her stomach, she walked over to Sean and asked him to dance.

"You're even more beautiful than you were in high school!" Sean whispered to her as they were dancing.

"Oh," she accused, "in high school, you didn't even know I existed."

"On the contrary," Sean corrected, "you were the love of my life. I was just too afraid to tell you. There wasn't an event that went by that I didn't wish you were my girl. You were so beautiful, so bright—and so reserved—I just knew you wouldn't go out with me. Our senior prom was the worst. I kept looking at you, wishing you were my date. There was one song, one special song that just broke my heart. It was 'Can I Have This Dance, for the Rest of My Life,' by Anne . . ."

". . . Murray," Katie said, finishing his sentence for him. "Yes," said Sean. "Do you know it?"

"Yes," was all she said.

My mother knows the story very well. You see, my mother's name is Katie. And Sean is my father. Later that long-ago evening, he asked the band to play "their song," and that's when he asked her to marry him.

It's a great love story. Even though this story ended happily, it's bittersweet, too, because my parents missed out on all those special times in high school when they wanted to share things with the other. They could have been "boyfriend and girlfriend" for those years, too.

My mother's story gave me the courage to ask Ben to the Sadie Hawkins dance at school.

P.S. He said yes!

—Stephanie Cohen, 16

My Friend, the Thief

When I was in the eighth grade, a girl named Mia spread a rumor that I was a "thief" because she believed that I had "stolen" from her. I don't know why she got all dramatic about it. I mean, all I did was take a cupful of grain from Mia's bag of horse food in the tack shed she and I shared at a stable where we both board our horses.

It's not like I wasn't going to replace the amount I'd taken. And, I would loan her grain if she needed it for her horse. Besides, all of us who boarded our horses there did this; it was a regular thing. And she knew that!

But Mia exaggerated the story and made me out to be a thief and spread the rumor throughout the entire school! She made it out like I belonged on the FBI's Most Wanted list.

The problem is, I didn't know the rumor was circulating throughout the school until one day when I was putting a note in my good friend's locker and a teacher coming down the hall saw me. The teacher began questioning me, asking to see what I had taken—as if I would steal something from my friend! Next thing I knew, girls in my gym class with lockers next to mine were glancing at me sideways, then shielding their locks from me, so I wouldn't see their combinations when they opened their lockers.

When I saw their mistrust, I knew they didn't see me as a friend.

It took me nearly four months for the rumor to die out. Not only did I have to regain the trust of a lot of people—trust I didn't deserve to lose in the first place—but I also had to put up with being treated with suspicion. It was the most terrible semester of school in my whole life.

I know how awful it feels to be the butt of a rumor. Because of the experience, I will never do it to someone else. I also know that I'll never believe that just because someone says something is true, that it means that it is true. I won't believe any rumor without absolute proof that it really happened just the way it's being told.

I've learned a really important lesson in friendship: If your classmates don't see you as a friend, they may well believe that worst about you.

—Sally Thornton, 14

"Cooler" Than You Think

When I was in junior high, Kent wasn't exactly the most popular guy in school. Actually, he was sort of a nerd. Hardly anyone talked to him—not for any particular reason, just nobody said much to him.

One day, after getting my lunch, I looked around for my friends in the cafeteria. They weren't there yet, and it was kind of crowded, so I took the first open seat I saw. I found myself sitting next to Kent. We started talking.

As it turns out, he's not so "different." In fact, Kent is a pretty smart guy. He's just quiet.

I was surprised to learn that he collects sports cards like I do. He even has a Ken Griffey Jr. rookie card—which is worth a couple hundred dollars—that he got from a three-dollar pack of cards! What luck! And, for his birthday this year, his uncle gave him a game-worn jersey card (that's one of the really cool cards that come with a small piece of the athlete's jersey right on the card). We had a really good conversation about where to find some good deals on some of the rare and hard-to-find cards. Kent told me he has both "Tough Stuff" and "Beckett" card books, which are the best ones to tell you what every card is worth.

While we were talking, we found out that we each have a couple of cards that the other wants. So now we're going to get together to compare our cards. He knows all about which ones are really hot and which ones are supposed to be going up in value. It's totally cool.

It just goes to show that sometimes people you don't know might be cooler than you think.

—Carl Galloway, 14

My two Best Friends are Very Different

Kayla and Sara are both friends of mine, but they're very different. For instance, the other day the three of us were going to go to the movies. "Do I look okay?" I asked Sara.

Without even so much as looking at me, she replied, "Yeah, sure. You always look great."

"How about my hair?"

"Yeah. Looks great," she responded.

The moment Kayla walked in, she took one look at me and demanded, "You're not going to be seen in that, are you?

"What's wrong with it?" I asked.

"Well, for one thing, you look like a little kid in it, and for another, there's a mustard stain on the left sleeve." She paused, frowned and then added, "Having a bad hair day?"

So you can see how different my two friends are. Sara is a person who doesn't want to upset you, so she always says something nice and would never want to make you feel uneasy, no matter what. Kayla is very blunt and outspoken. She has very definite opinions and isn't afraid to be honest. Kayla is definitely not afraid of what you'll think about what she has to say.

So, if I really, really want to know how I look, while I ask them both, it's Kayla's advice that's worth the most. If the way I look passes her inspection, I can be sure that it will pass with others.

Now, if I was worried about a big test at school,

I'd go to Sara for help. Kayla puts as little energy as possible into her grades. Sara, on the other hand, is very smart, understands what it's like to want to get good grades, and will help you out when you need it. So both Kayla and Sara are good friends, each in her own way.

Friends. They're so different. That's why you need lots of them.

—**Barbara Allen, 14**

I Threw His Note Back at Him

I remember the night my boyfriend and I broke up. We went to a movie, and on the way home I mentioned that I was planning to get a new dress for the big school dance that was coming up. I asked him what he thought he was going to wear. That's when he told me he couldn't take me to the dance. That really upset me. And frustrated me. I really, really liked him, but I often found myself without a date for many of the special things going on. If he was my boyfriend, my only boyfriend, why wouldn't he want to take me to all the many things going on?

By the time we reached my house, I was even more upset. Thinking that we wouldn't be going to the big dance upset me so much that I didn't even wait for him to finish what he was saying. I got out of the car, and as I was slamming the door, I hollered, "Well fine. If you don't take me, then I don't want to go out with you anymore. We're through!"

Later that night, he called and asked, "Can we talk?" "No!" I yelled and hung up.

The next day at school he walked over to me while I was at my locker and tried handing me a note. I was still mad, so I grabbed the note and threw it back at him. Looking sad, he just walked away.

I picked up the note so none of the other kids

who saw it fall to the floor would read it, and tossed it in my history book—where it stayed on the top shelf of my locker for the next several days. I was just miserable.

Sitting at home—the night after the dance—I took my history book from my backpack, retrieved his letter and read it.

Dear Connie,

I'm sorry I can't take you to all the things that I'd like to. I'd love to take you everywhere—to every dance, every movie, to the fair when it comes to town, to restaurants. I don't know how to tell you this and still be fair to you, but it's just that most of the money I earn from my part-time job goes to help my mother pay our bills. She works hard to take care of me and my brother and sister, but she can't do it alone. I love being with you. . . . going places and doing all the little things that make you happy, I just can't afford to right now.

I miss you. . . . you know that we should be together. I know how important it is to you to go to the school dance. If you don't mind that I don't rent a tux, if you don't mind that the corsage I give you isn't made of the orchids I know you deserve, then I'd love to take you to the dance. I miss you so much. Please reconsider.

Love,
Kurt

My heart aches because of the way I treated

Kurt. He is such a good guy and I really hurt him—all because I refused to listen.

The irony is that because I wouldn't communicate, I ended up hurting myself, too.

I'm a better listener now and I don't jump to conclusions so fast. That's been helpful, too!

And, I now read notes my friends give me the instant I receive them!

—Connie Hunt, 16

Sometimes You Just Outgrow Your Friends

My older sister is in her first year of junior college and having a great time. It's all she talks about. So I've decided I want to go to college, too—the same one she's attending.

I haven't always wanted to go to college. My two best friends, Lindy and Rianna, and I had planned to find jobs and share an apartment right after we got out of high school. Now that my plans have changed, I have a bit of a problem. For one thing, my grades haven't been all that great, so I'm going to have to put more time into my school studies to make sure I can get accepted to college. This means I'm going to have to spend less time with Lindy and Rianna. I'm no longer as interested in being a high school student, as I am in becoming a college student.

Lindy and Rianna and I have always spent nearly all our free time together. We go to the arcade every day after school, and sometimes on the weekends. If we're not there, we're at the movies—or somewhere. Lindy and Rianna are a lot of fun to be with. Even so, being with them takes up a lot of my time. While this was once okay, now it's more time than I'm willing to give up. So the problem is, now that our lives are starting to go in different directions, the friendship is really strained. I'm beginning to spend more time with my sister—and her friends.

At first Lindy and Rianna were okay with this, now they seem annoyed. They say things like,

"Are you going with us to the movies on Friday, or are you going to hang out with your preppie friends?" "What do you mean, you can't go? It's only homework," or "Don't be such a drag."

I think that when you change, your friends have a hard time with it. Sometimes you can't prevent hard feelings. The sad truth is, sometimes you just outgrow your friends.

—**Belinda Carr, 16**

Anything . . . for Friends

I worked long and hard at getting accepted by the group of guys I hang out with—Jared, Todd, Dennis and Greg. I'd do anything for them. When they all took karate, I took karate, too. At first, most of them were better at it than I was, but I kept at it and practiced my moves. I wanted to show them I could hold my own with them. And I did.

When they all got skateboards, I got one, too. We do some pretty cool stunts with them. I learned how to handle my board better than anyone else. I'm not just saying that, you could ask any of them.

Being their friend means a lot to me. I'd do anything for them. Like when Todd asked me to get the answers to the second-period math test, I said, "No problem." I got the answers for him. That's what friends do. They do things for each other; they especially help one another out when they need it. At least that's what I thought!

Then, last week my skateboard got trashed when I was going over this really huge ramp, and it shot away from under me. I wasn't hurt, but my skateboard was totaled. So I asked Todd if I could use his. He said, "No way, I want to keep my board in one piece." I asked Jared and Dennis and Greg, too. They all laughed and said just about the same thing. I couldn't believe it because I'd let them at least have some time using my skateboard if the same thing had happened to theirs. But not one of them would do it for me.

Maybe my sister was right. She said I shouldn't have to keep proving myself with my friends.

—**Mike Madson, 13**

Making Friends with the "Once Missing" Parts of Me

A while ago
I was feeling lonely and lost
Living in a frenetic and impersonal world
Never quite feeling like I belonged.

Something was missing
But what could it be?
It couldn't be God, friends, boyfriend, or family—
I had all that.

Then one day I figured it out.
The emptiness was inside,
I was missing the full sense of me.
A self too narrowly defined, I had no friendship with me,
Limiting—because there are so many sides to me.

I have my share of tears and fears,
Even doubts and insecurities.
I'm capable of greatness—and goof-ups, too.
I am a princess wishing for a big stone castle,
I am an Olympic champion with silver, bronze and gold;
I am a daughter, sister, cousin, student and friend.

I've claimed all the "once missing" parts of me.
—**Danyalle Williams, 16**

The Difference Between a Friend and a Best Friend

I have a couple of good friends. One of them, Berneice Long, is my *best* friend. Last Tuesday was her last day at school. Berneice said that they had to move away because her father took a job in another town.

I don't think I'll ever see my friend again, and that is such a sad feeling.

My two other friends and I live only a couple of blocks from school, so every day we walk home together. Usually we talk about some of the things that happened in school that day, like if someone in our class got called on and they didn't know the right answer or said something really weird or stupid. My friends and I always talk about who wore what (especially if that person got something new) and how she looked in it. We tell each other if we've heard a new rumor (and who started it, or, who we think started it), and we go over the current status of an old rumor.

There's so much to talk about that we barely cover everything before we part ways. Then, we call each other when we get home and talk some more. It's great to have friends!

On the way home from school yesterday we didn't talk about the things we usually do. Yesterday, all we talked about was our friend Berneice, and how sad we were about her leaving and how much we

were going to miss her. And we all cried. We were so
sad that we actually just stopped walking because
we needed to wipe away our tears.

Seeing how sad each of us was, we just stood
there for a couple of minutes, held hands, hugged,
and then cried some more. Finally, because all we
could manage was to cry, dry our eyes, cry some
more and then wipe away some more tears, we all
started to laugh. That made us feel much better so
then we started walking again. The rest of the way
we just talked about how nice Berneice was, and
how we hoped we would all get to see her again.

We all agreed she was a good friend, a "best
friend."

I guess that when you're feeling as much hurt
over one particular person as we are over our friend
moving away, you know that the person was really
a good friend—and a very special person. I mean,
I've had other friends move away but I didn't cry
over them.

My older sister's friend once told me that if you
break up with a boyfriend and you don't cry, then
it means it really wasn't true love—that the boy was
more of a friend than a boyfriend. So, if crying over
a friend is proof that that person is a best friend
and not just a friend, then for sure Berneice is a best
friend.

That day, as we parted ways, the three of us

promised each other that if any one of us were ever to move away, we'd all feel this very same way toward the one who left. We agreed on something else, too. We were all now more than just friends.

We had become "best" friends.

—**Meghan Smith, 12**

"With Ears Like That, You Must Have to Hide During Rabbit-Hunting Season!"

"Look at the way she walks with that ugly brown back! She looks like a camel!" my friend in said loudly as we strolled into the Girls' bathroom. Kim was talking about Tamara D., one of our classmates who was walking into the bathroom in front of us. I don't know why she said it. I mean, she doesn't even know Tamara all that well. But comparing the brown backpack to a camel was sort of funny to me so I laughed right along with Kim. But I also laughed for another reason: Kim is my friend, and she expects me to be loyal.

Then, Kim made yet another snide remark, this one directly to a girl new to our school (whose name is Nina Nguyen) who was with Tamara. As Nina looked in the mirror at her hair, which she was wearing up, Kim met my eyes in the mirror and said, "With big ears like those, can you believe she'd wear her hair up like that?"

Frankly, I thought the style was kind of cute on her, and the truth is, Nina's ears aren't all that big, so I couldn't believe Kim made this remark—and so loud. Then, Kim looked straight at Nina in the mirror said, and "You must have to hide during rabbit-hunting season, huh?"

I glanced at Nina's stricken face then glanced away really quick. I knew the comment hurt Nina's feelings.

I was really in a bind. It's not a good feeling when you know a remark has hurt someone—even if the remark is a funny one. The thing is, what's a friend supposed to do? I mean, Kim makes snide remarks all the time, and sometimes what she says is really funny. But when she says it in front of the person—that's just mean.

This time, I just stood, there being silent—which obviously upset Kim. "Hey!" she called out, elbowing me to remind me I was supposed to say something in support of her. Instead, I said "Yeah, I heard you, but it's not even true." My heart was pounding because it's hard to stand up to a friend who might dump you.

That's the hard part about having friends. Sometimes they do and say stupid things, and you're just supposed to back them up. Sometimes when we have discussions in Life-Skills class, we talk about things like this. And everyone has all the "right" answers; they say all the words that sound right. But the truth is, when you don't back up your friend, she's going to get back at you, there will be a time when YOU are going to be the butt of her joke. That would be so embarrassing.

Anyway, Kim was upset that I hadn't backed her up. She rolled her eyes and shook her head and said snidely, "Whatever!" The first time she saw me alone she thanked me; it was a very nice feeling.

Friends! From the moment you enter kindergarten, you think that friends are the most important thing in the entire world. But the moment you have friends, things get complicated.

Right now, I'd say that having friends keeps you busy guessing what they'll do next. Don't get me wrong; I don't want to be without friends. That would be awful; it's just that having friends is, well, like being a rabbit in rabbit-hunting season: there are times when you'd like to find a place to hide!

—**Janice Langsworth, 16**

Are You a Friend or Foe?

Wondering as I sit here alone in my room
My feelings so sad, all doom and gloom.
I think about us, the bond between me and you—
How you're my friend, but a real foe, too.

Your "on-again, off-again" confuses me to no end,
You say you're sorry, and you'll make amends.
When I share with others how perplexed I feel,
They say, "Maybe your friendship just isn't for real."

Maybe they're right: It's a double-lane road,
Your being two-faced is such a burdensome load.
Mostly I can't stand the way you gossip around,
Always loving the mean-spirited news you've just found.

I'm afraid if I tell you I've had my fill,
You'll give me that look, and a silence to kill,
Then there'll be consequences to pay,
And I'll be compromising; I hate feeling this way!

I'd like to tell you, have the truth be known,
About my feelings—an interest you've never shown.
Giving wings to my words is a very big help
What a relief to give in to the things that I've felt.

I know you've noticed we've grown apart,
More foes than friends, so we've got to start
To talk about us, about you and me
I think you'll see this is no way to be.

So how about it, when can we start,
To find a new way to talk heart-to-heart,
To bring back the warmth we used to share
Cause deep down inside, I know we both care.

—Elizabeth Martone, 16

"Think Team!"

I knew that my mom and dad were serious about moving from Chicago to Houston when, the moment school let out for spring vacation, we all piled in the car and left for Houston. Probably so that we wouldn't feel so bad over having to leave behind our friends—and basically, give up our lives as we knew them—our parents asked my brother and me if there was one "special requirement" each of us would like our new house to have.

I have always wanted a bay window, and my brother wanted a yard big enough to kick around a soccer ball.

My parents thought that sounded good, too, and said we'd try to find a house with a "little personality"—hopefully one with a bay window and a big yard.

My brother was upset that we were leaving Chicago. He had a lot of friends and played sports.

I was happy to leave Chicago! I didn't really have a lot of friends at all and in fact, was sure that the kids at school didn't like me. I was constantly called a "teacher's pet" and a "suck-up." The only explanation I could think of for calling me these names was they must be jealous of the good grades I got. I've always been a straight-A student. And, I am polite and have good manners; I'm also quiet and shy. I was looking forward to going to school somewhere else. Moving didn't seem like a losing proposition to me: I was glad to say good-bye!

Once in Houston, we stayed with my aunt. Each day we got up early and along with my aunt and cousin, we'd drive around to see all different types of houses. My brother was bored to tears, but I didn't think of it as all that bad because I got to hang out with my older cousin, Ashley, who is very cool. Besides, inside the model and open house homes we looked through, there were free sodas, donuts and cookies (and sometimes bowls of mixed candies). Since we were told we could help ourselves, we did!

By the second weekend of June, my family had found the house we were going to live in. It was brand-new—and yes, with a big yard and a bay window in the living room! But since our house wasn't going to be completed for a couple of months, it meant we had to stay with my aunt for longer than we had planned.

When school time rolled around, we were still living with my aunt and uncle, so my mom signed my brother and me up to go to school where my cousins went to school. I was happy to be going back because I've always liked school.

Unlike my school in Chicago, this school had a "Cooperative Learning" curriculum—which is basically a philosophy of "think team" (the teachers' words)—which means that the learning and studying is done in groups of three to five students. This also means that there's no such thing as an individual grade: You get a "group grade," and everyone in the group receives the same grade. It's a fun way to learn—and a great way to know other students, so I was having a good time.

Then, about two months later, my family learned that our house was ready. Our new house was on the other side of town so after the move we'd be going to a school closer to our new home. I was disappointed to have to leave this school, because I liked it so much. Nevertheless, the next week I enrolled in my new school.

While my goal was still to be a good student, I hoped to make friends. I decided to try out what I'd learned from the head teacher of the Cooperative Learning curriculum who had said, "It's not just about you; think team." I'd say "think team" is a good approach to making friends—or at least it's working for me. Basically, that means I remember that other people count, and I should do my part to reach out and be friendly.

When I think back to my having friends in Chicago, I think it's fair to say that I expected to have friends simply "because." Then, when no one really knew me, I blamed it on their being jealous because I got good grades. Now I know that had nothing to do with it. Here at this school, I'm still smart, still a good student, the teachers like me—and I have friends!

—Lindsay Moody, 15

The Illegal U-Turn

I live one mile from my school. That's not a long way, really, but still, I absolutely detest having to walk to school, especially in the mornings. My parents argue that walking to and from school is "good for my health," so unless I'm running late or have something special going on before or after school, they're not likely to give me a ride. So, as often as I can, I mooch rides from friends who drive, especially from my friend Kenny, who has a monstrously rad Ford truck. "Can I catch a ride home with you after sixth period?" I asked him one day last year. "No problem," my newest best friend assured me.

Just like the other kids who have wheels, Kenny has a lot of friends eager to catch a ride somewhere. So if you get lucky and he's still got space, you need to get to his truck early if you want a good seat—like a window seat or, best of all, the front seat. Sitting there is on a first-come, first-served basis.

I prefer the front seat, so as soon as the bell rang, I sprinted from my class to Kenny's truck in hopes of getting the front seat. Even though I hurried, when I got to his truck, his sister, Cyndi, had already claimed the front seat. "You always get the front seat. How about giving it up just this once?" I coaxed.

"If you let me sit here today, I promise I won't ask you for it again for a whole month." It worked. She scooted in the back seat, and I climbed in and buckled up. I wasn't about to give up my "real estate" to anyone else who had also been promised a ride. There were five of us total. Kenny counted heads, and off we went.

Taking his usual route, Kenny headed down the street and made a left turn at the stop sign. Soaring along, Kenny drove right past the turn he needed to make to drop off his first passenger. Realizing his mistake, Kenny decided right then and there to turn around! The problem is, rather than going to the end of the street to make a proper turn, Kenny looked over his shoulder to check on the oncoming traffic, and then proceeded to make an illegal U-turn. Surprised—and feeling ill at ease—I, too, glanced over my shoulder, and noticed a dark-blue Ford Bronco coming right at us at a very high speed! Then, in the very next moment, about the same time I yelled to Kenny about the oncoming truck, the Bronco was on us.

There was the incredible sound of the two automobiles crashing and sliding, and Cyndi screaming. The Bronco smashed into Kenny's truck on the driver's side, pushing our car into a wild slide, while the impact caused the Bronco to go airborne. The Bronco then landed with a thud, bounced, rolled and landed on its hood, skidding twenty-some feet, then flipping once again on its side and sliding into the nearby curb—which caused it to flip once again before it finally skidded to a dead halt, facing the opposite direction. Talk about scary!

After a quick panicked search to see if the passengers in our truck were okay (they were), I knew I'd better get over to the Bronco to see if anyone needed help. Though Kenny's truck had been brutally hit, it was now upright. Even so, the impact had jammed the car door on my side, so I rolled down the window, climbed out and ran over to the Bronco. Thankfully, everyone was alive, but two of its three passengers needed emergency medical care. I ran across the street to the closest professional building and was told that help had already been called and was on the way. I raced back to the scene of the accident.

Within minutes, police and paramedics arrived and one of the passengers was life-flighted by helicopter to the nearest hospital. As for the passengers in our car, Cyndi didn't have her seat belt on and was thrown into the front seat. Thankfully, she was okay. Like the others, I had my seat belt on, so while I was a little sore from being yanked by the force of my seat belt holding me in place, I was okay. The driver's side of Kenny's truck sustained the direct hit of the Bronco, but incredibly, Kenny didn't have any injuries whatsoever. The two other friends in the car were both okay also.

After the immediate commotion of the car crash was over, Kenny and I sat on the grass, waiting for our parents to come and get us, just staring at his badly damaged truck and what was left of the

Bronco. Still scared from our ordeal, Kenny and I talked about what had happened and what we were feeling. We recounted every detail of the crash, and admitted how scared it made us; we even described the rusty taste of adrenaline we felt when we saw the Bronco was right on us.

Then we talked about the consequences of what had just happened, like the illegal U-turn, and how if Cyndi had been wearing her seat belt, it might have prevented her from being thrown into the front seat. She was lucky she wasn't injured. And we talked about what was going to happen next. I wasn't exactly forbidden to get a ride home from school, but my parents made it clear they preferred that I walked home. As a licensed driver, Kenny was at fault in the accident and had totaled his truck. For sure Kenny would have some explaining to do to his parents!

It was a good talk. We both were still so frightened and so concerned for everyone, including facing the consequences of all this, that we didn't hesitate to be honest about how we were feeling. In fact, it was one of the most "real" conversations I remember having with another guy friend—one that made us feel close to each other. It also established us as *real* friends. For the rest of the school year, Kenny and I found ourselves drawn together out of a certain commonality. Whenever we found ourselves in the same activity or study group at school, we instantly clicked, as if we had been lifelong buddies. We became such good friends that, right now, I'd say he's my closest friend.

It was the discussion that made all the difference. I think the main reason we got so close is not just because we went through a very frightening ordeal together, but because we opened up and talked about it with total honesty. It was our frank and open discussion that cemented a friendship that's deeper than most of my other friendships.

From this incident, I've learned an important ingredient in friendships: "Real" conversations make friendships stronger and your importance to each other greater. And of course, I'm certain that I will NEVER make an illegal U-Turn.

—Curt Lindholm, 17

Needed: Body Parts

A friend:

A brain to pick
A shoulder to cry on
Ears to hear all
An arm to rely on
Eyes to reflect hope
A voice to give cheer
A hand strong to hold
A heart that's sincere
Someone who cares
A soul you can share.
A friend.

—Jennifer Leigh, 20

Sticks and Stones . . .

Do you believe the saying: "Sticks and stones can break my bones, but words can never hurt me"? I don't.

I think words are very powerful, and while they may not break your bones, they can break your heart. Consider the words,"I love you."Just these three short words can change your life when someone says them to you. Just like the words "I hate you."They definitely have the power to hurt you. So I think words can sometimes be as forceful and have as much effect on a person as actions. I should know; I experienced this firsthand.

My friend Brenda Hall couldn't seem to accept that her boyfriend and I could be platonic friends. But we were. Tom and I had been friends even longer than Brenda and I had—and we'd all been friends since grade school. But when she and Tom broke up, for some weird reason, she thought it was because of me, but it wasn't because of me. I didn't do one thing to cause them to break up, nor did I want Tom for a boyfriend—as Brenda must have thought. In fact, once Brenda and Tom weren't together, he started dating another girl at our school, Leeza Nero.

You would think that would be the end of Brenda's being upset with me, and I wouldn't be blamed as the reason for the breakup after that. But for some reason, Tom's liking another girl made Brenda even more furious at *me*. So the very next day after she saw Tom and Leeza together, she started a rumor that she'd seen me flirting with a guy at school. I thought I would die of embarrassment.

Even though I knew my close friends didn't believe such terrible gossip, my life was still ruined. I was sure the rumor would travel very quickly throughout the entire school. Luckily, I learned about the rumor during the last period of the day, and after that I could just go home. But how would I make it through the next day . . . and the next? All I could do was think about having such a dreadful scandal circulating throughout the school about me—and started by a "friend"! Some friend. I woke up sure that words could hurt as much as "sticks and stones," and I was certain my broken heart hurt every bit as much as any broken bone could.

The next day I went to school miserable, knowing that all day long everyone was going to be hearing the disgraceful lie. In my first-period homeroom, I settled in my desk and stared down at my notebook so I wouldn't have to meet either the looks of pity from classmates who didn't believe the rumor, or the smirks and leers of those who did. I could hardly wait for this day to end. I was even considering going to the nurse's office and saying I was sick, which, given how I felt, wouldn't be such a big stretch. I had an enormous headache, and my stomach was positively turned upside down. I decided that just as soon as morning announcements were over,

I'd head to the nurse's office. But then something unexpected happened.

Each morning, right after the principal greets the students and announces what, if anything, is urgent for us kids to know, there is an "inspirational" message read by a student. This always follows the announcements. One by one, everyone in the school has to read one, and we were now up to the H's; it was Brian Holt's turn to read something today. Yet, surprisingly enough, Brian Holt didn't read the message. Instead, Gina Issacks (who would normally follow Brian Holt) read it.

"Hi," she began. "I'm Gina Issacks and this morning I'd like to read a message that I think relates to a lot of things going on around school. I think you'll get my drift. Here goes: A man came to a rabbi and said, 'Oh, Rabbi, I have done wrong. I have slandered a friend. I have told lies about him. I have spread rumors. But now I am sorry for what I have done and what I have said. How can I be forgiven?' The rabbi looked thoughtfully at the man and then said, 'Take this feather pillow and go to the town square. Cut the pillow open and let the feathers fly to the wind. That will be your punishment for the ill words you have spoken.' Though quite puzzled by the rabbi's instructions, the man did as he was told. Then he returned to the rabbi and said, 'I have done what you told me. Now am I forgiven for slandering my friend?'

'No, you are not forgiven yet,' the rabbi replied. 'You have fulfilled only half of your task. First you let the feathers fly to the wind. Now go and collect every single feather.'

"I think it's a great parable. When you think about how important it is to be a good friend and to be considerate of the feelings of our friends, then you shouldn't start rumors that aren't true, or say things that are hurtful." Gina paused a moment, as if giving her words time to sink in, then finished by saying, "Enough said."

This warm feeling of relief just seeped through my heart. I had to fight back tears, I was so touched that someone cared enough to stick up for me. Gina isn't one of my close friends, but she's considered a nice girl throughout the school. I'm sure she read this piece either for Brenda's benefit, or because the rumor about me was by now going around like wildfire. Reading the parable was an attempt to quash it.

Whatever the intent, I was thankful. Even better news is that right after homeroom, Brenda met me at my locker and apologized for being mad at me over her and Tom breaking up, as well as for starting the rumor. Though she didn't say if her change of heart had anything to do with Gina's reading, she did promise to make sure everyone knew that what she said wasn't true.

So I forgave her and said we could still be friends. And speaking of friends, real friends, I knew I'd always be grateful to Gina who used the power of her words to help friends be real friends. That's why

Gina is now one of my best friends!
—**Audrianne Adams, 16**

Do You Miss Me?

Hello Grandpa!
I just wanted to say,
I love you and miss you
And wish you had stayed.

You were my best friend,
A friend pure as gold
My most favorite best friend,
If the whole truth be told.

Do you miss me?
Can you feel the pain in my heart?
I'd like to believe
We're not really far apart.

I'm playing my music,
It always brings me to tears
If only we'd been together,
For a couple more years.

I love how you listened,
How we'd sing you and I.
Since you now sing with angels,
Do you see how I cry?

Know that I miss you,
And I need you still
Even if you're in heaven,
Know that I always will.

So keep watch over me Grandpa,
My very best friend,
And know that I'll always love you,
You're the truest of friends.

—**Jenna King, 12**

"It'll Never Get to Us"

It started out like a typical day, but turned out to be anything but typical. As usual, I went to school and sat through my eighth-grade classes, then came home with mounds of homework. And, as usual, I prepared to put off doing it for as long as possible. Little did I know, I would soon have every excuse to put off getting it done.

The neighborhood was stirring with talk of a fire burning in our direction. Filled with curiosity—and alarm—my mom, brother and I walked to the top of the street to survey the situation and get a better idea of whether or not there was any possible danger. Looking out to the hills behind my house, we saw a wall of orange flames, set against a background of ominous, thick, black smoke. My mother and the other adults that had gathered there tried to reassure us kids, as well as each other. "It's so far away," someone offered, while another one said, "It'll never get to us." But I could tell that they were only trying to reassure us and convince themselves. We kids grew worried—because we could see our parents were. Everyone fretted over the flames growing closer, as if being annoyed and upset might somehow hold back this fiery mower that was eating its way through the brush towards us.

"You know, maybe we should pack up our things . . . just in case," someone soon ventured. I looked up at my mother, and she nodded kind of stiffly and agreed, "Yes, better to be safe than sorry.

So we went back to our house to pack up our belongings "just in case"—to be "safe" rather than "sorry." In the next split-second everyone left, like all they needed was someone to give them permission to be downright scared of the fire coming in our direction.

"Just take the basic necessities and valuables!" my mother instructed. Rushing into my room, I looked around in a panic, trying to decide what to take. Other than one bulletin board I'd trashed and wanted to replace, everything there was "basic necessities and valuables" to me. It was so hard to pick and choose what I would save and what I wouldn't.

Soon my dad got home from work and joined in the packing frenzy. In no time we had both cars loaded to the brim with picture albums, journals, family keepsakes and, of course, our dog. By now police cars were driving down our street, telling us on their loudspeakers to evacuate our houses. My dad stood with a hose on the roof of our house, trying to water it down, as the wall of fire seemed to march like a deadly infantry of flames down the hills in our direction. My mom kept yelling up at my dad to get down off the roof so we could leave.

"Take the kids and go! I'll meet you somewhere!" he hollered back at her.

"No! I'm not leaving you!" she shouted in reply. Finally, my dad could see that she meant it—we wouldn't leave without him. So, he got down from the roof. As we drove away from the house, we were all somber and silent. It was the strangest feeling, because I didn't know if I would have a house to come back to.

After dinner at a local restaurant with some of our neighbors and several other evacuated families, we spent the night at a friend's house. For once in my life, I wanted to do my homework. . . . I wanted everything to be normal again. But we just stayed awake and watched the news coverage of the fire. For someone who doesn't like to get up in the morning, I was awake at 5:30—and then discovered that everyone else was already in the process of getting dressed. We all wanted to return home—to see if we still had one.

Lucky for us, our house was untouched by the fire. As happy as we were that our home was okay, we were saddened to see that our friends at the end of the street weren't as fortunate. Their home was burned to the ground. Standing there assessing the neighborhood, emotions from gratitude to sorrow flooded my mind. I was thankful that I had my home and all my things to come home to, and thankful that no one was hurt from this disastrous fire. And I considered how terrible it must feel for those who lost everything they owned. And I was filled with a deep, overall appreciation for life—for being alive, and for just everything.

The idea that fire could claim lives just as it had homes made me especially grateful for having both a home and a family. Having watched each member of my family grab the things that were valuable to them—things that were basic, and the little mementos that were so precious to each person— filled me with a special appreciation for each of them. We were a family—a real family. And now, a safe one.

Right then and there I made a pact with myself never to take for granted the things that can be swept away in an instant, like your home and possessions—and the life of family members.

The experience left me with a new sense of the importance of family, and for sure, a new sense of meaning behind my mother's words, "the basic necessities and valuables." My parents and my brother, and the close relationships we share as a family, are definitely basic necessities and my most treasured valuables in life. My family members are also among the closest and most precious friends I have.

—Carrie Hague, 17

New—and Late

There's someone who is different
As different as she can be
She's walking into my classroom
I pray she'll sit by me.

Like me, she is wearing braces
Her hair is black and straight
Dark eyes look at our faces
She knows she's new—and late.

Our curious eyes are on her
Most staring blank and grim
But my eyes are open and hopeful
My heart invites her in.

And in that aching moment
When throats feel dry and tight
I'll volunteer to help her
And make her first day right.

—Leslie Hendrickson, 13

The Mystery Letter

My little brother was diagnosed as having an inoperable brain tumor. There was nothing anyone could do except enjoy every second Stevie had left to live. It was a sad time, but it was a special time, too.

Stevie believed in God and told everyone he wasn't afraid because he knew he was going to heaven. He even wrote letters to God expecting God to write back. Well of course, no one wanted to tell a sick little boy that God didn't write letters, so no one did.

Then one day, a letter from God did come for Stevie. My mother gave it to Stevie, and he read it to us: God said he was reading every one of Stevie's letters and was watching over our family. Stevie kept writing. And God kept answering! Stevie found great comfort from these letters.

Stevie died six months later. Though it seemed like he had been ill forever, it was only ten months from the time he learned he had the brain tumor until the time he died. But during those ten months, our family was closer and more loving than it had ever been.

The day after Stevie's funeral the mailman knocked on our door and handed my mother a shoebox filled with the letters Stevie had written to God. Seeing Stevie's devotion in writing so many letters to God, the mailman had taken it upon himself to bring comfort, encouragement and hope to my little brother by answering his letters to God.

I guess some people would say it takes a lot of nerve to play God, but in this case, I think it took a lot of heart. I think it's a cool thing for the mailman to have done; he befriended a little boy going through the roughest time imaginable.

I can't help but think how happy all of us in the world could make each other if we were the kind of friends the mailman was to Stevie—and if we would encourage and comfort each other.

—Bill Lempke, 15

Bonham

When I was twelve, my mother and father divorced. It seemed like after that, my life just fell apart. My mother and I moved into a smaller house in a different neighborhood. Because of the move, I had to go to a new school. Leaving my friends was the pits. At first, I didn't know anybody and felt really out of place. Since my mother doesn't get home from work until around 7:00, and because I hadn't made any new friends at school yet, I didn't have anyone to hang out with, so I just went home.

With only me there, the house seemed really spooky. I'd put the TV on and play my music, but then I started going to the nearby arcade just to hang around. It wasn't too long before I began hanging out with a couple of kids who were always there. Unfortunately, the two who were the most friendly had dropped out of school. But they were fun guys, and I looked forward to seeing them after school. As soon as the last bell rang, I'd head straight to the arcade. Sometimes I stayed there later than my mother allowed, and we began to get into arguments about it. She said if I continued to hang out with my new friends, they'd get me into trouble.

Then, one weekend when I was staying with my father, out of the blue, he gave me a dog, a golden retriever, one who already had a name, "Bonham." Dad let me take Bonham home to my mother's with me and bring him on the weekends when I visited him.

Obviously he had talked this over with my mother, because she welcomed the dog without complaining about having Bonham in our house. That really surprised me, because Mom didn't necessarily like animals, especially living in the house. I'd wanted a hamster and she said it was too messy; I'd asked for a bunny and she said it was too smelly. But she seemed to welcome Bonham. She even put up the little knickknacks from the coffee table because Bonham would be so happy all the time, he would swish his big tail and all the little figurines would go flying. One of my mother's favorite ones, a little glass kangaroo broke in a gazillion pieces. She was upset, but then, when Bonham saw her huddled on the floor gathering up the little pieces, he ran over and licked her face, and she couldn't help laughing. And she wasn't upset after that.

But it's more than just that Bonham is fun to have around and is a great friend. He's really changed how I feel about coming home after school. It may sound dumb for me to call Bonham my friend, but he really is. You may not believe that a dog can have such a big effect on a person's life, but Bonham has on mine. He needs me and depends on me. When I get home from school, he's waiting right there for me. He knows exactly when to expect me. He's really cute about it, too. He'll stand on his hind legs and put his paws on the window sill, and when he sees me coming into view, he starts barking. Then he runs to greet me at the door. It's a great feeling. Bonham jumps on my bed when I put my stuff away; he sits on the couch with me when I watch television; and when I fix dinner, he's right there. I'm really important to him.

And he's really important to me, too. I take him with me for walks. I know it sounds silly but I really think he knows what I'm saying, because if I ask him a question, he looks at me, cocks his head and barks! Bonham is the reason I come home immediately after school instead of hanging out with the kids I used to get into trouble with. Bonham depends on me to take him outdoors. He depends on me for food and water, and for companionship, too. Right now I'd say that he is just about the best friend I have. He's probably the best friend I've ever had. I love him very much. I am so happy my father gave him to me.

Bonham taught me that it isn't so bad being responsible; it actually brings out the best in you. Because of what Bonham taught me about the importance of being a friend who can be counted on, I've also learned to make friends who I can count on. Today my friends can count on me not to get them in trouble, and I can count on the same from them. So, I'd have to say my friendship with Bonham taught me how to be a better friend to everyone—to my parents, to my new friends and even to myself.

—Randy Candenwell, 14

CHAPTER 3

MY PERSONAL WORKBOOK: HOW TO BE A GOOD FRIEND

Do you ever "play into" or portray an image you believe someone else holds of you even though it's "not you"? For example, do you wear your hair in a certain style (or color) or dress or behave in a certain way because you think someone else will like you better if you do?

The Paintbrush

I keep my paintbrush with me, wherever I may go,
In case I need to cover up, so the real me doesn't show.
I'm so afraid to show you me; afraid of what you'll do,
I'm afraid you'll laugh or say mean things; afraid I might lose you.

I'd like to remove all the layers, to show you the real, true me,
But I want you to try to understand; I need you to like what you see.

So if you'll be patient and close your eyes, I'll remove the coats real slow,
Please understand how much it hurts, to let the
real me show.

Now that my coats are all stripped off, I feel na-
ked, bare and cold,
And if you still find me pleasing, you are my
friend, pure as gold.
I need to save my paintbrush though, and hold it
in my hand,
I need to keep it handy in case someone doesn't
understand.

So please protect me, my dear friend, and thanks
for loving me true,
And please let me keep my paintbrush with me,
Until I love me, too.

                                        —Lee Ezell

What is your paintbrush—how do you "cover up"
when you need to?

_____

_____

Decisions: An Identity of Your Own

Describe a time when you "covered up" who you are in order to gain someone's acceptance or approval. What did you do? What were you covering up? What "image" were you trying to present? Whose acceptance or approval were you trying to win?

_____

_____

_____

Did it work—was that person impressed? Did he or she like you better as a result of the image you presented?

_____

_____

Did you "fool" that person into thinking you were who you represented? How do you know? How did you feel about the whole thing? If you fooled someone, how did this make you feel about that person?

_____

_____

Why did you feel you had to act in a way other than your authentic self?

_____

_____

What Do You Think About Me?
Do You Accept Me as I Am?

It's only natural to want to be liked and accepted by others. Though we may not always ask aloud, we are always wondering:

"Do you think I'm okay?"

"Do you like the way I look?"

"Do you approve of how I act?"

"Do you like me?"

"Do you accept me as I am?"

"Do you like the way I dress?"

"Will you stick by me in good times and bad?"

"Will you be my friend—always?"

What else would you add to this list?

❤ _____

❤ _____

❤ _____

We want the answer to each of these questions to be an enthusiastic "Yes!" When others like us and accept us, we feel valued—like we're a terrific person. And that's a good feeling. Who, more than anyone else, makes you feel like a "terrific" person?

_____

_____

Knowing others is intelligence;
knowing yourself is true wisdom.

—**Tao Te Ching**

What does that person do to make you feel so good about yourself, so special? For example: Does he or she support you in being your best? Is he or she patient with you? Does he or she give you the benefit of the doubt? Does he or she trust you? Is he or she a good listener, one who always pays close attention to what you say? Does he or she respect your opinion even if it is different than his or her own?

List two things that person says or does that make you feel like a terrific person.

1. _____

_____

2. _____

_____

How does this "positive review" contribute to the image you hold of yourself?

_____

_____

Who counts on you to see him or her as being special?

_____

_____

What two things do you do that create a positive picture for that person?

1. _____

_____

2. _____

_____

Who I Am . . . Accept Me as I Am . . .

Even though we may want to feel accepted by others, it doesn't always work out that way. Sometimes this doesn't bother us, but most of the time, especially if their approval is important to us, we feel rejected, hurt or left out. It's only natural to feel this way.

Write about a time when you really wanted a certain person to think well of you and it just didn't happen. Who was the person? How long had you been hoping to gain this person's friendship before you realized there wasn't much of a chance? Why didn't he or she "like" you? How do you know if this was really the case? How did not gaining this person's friendship or acceptance make you feel about yourself? How did it make you feel about the other person?

_____

_____

_____

_____

Do you think it's important to always work toward getting others to like us? How important is it to you?

_____

_____

When someone doesn't like you as much as you would like them to, how does it change the way you feel about yourself?

_____

_____

What do you do when someone doesn't like you as much as you would like? For example, do you write that person a letter telling him or her about your feelings? Or do you go on about your business, reminding yourself that you have other friends and focusing on being a good friend to them—and to yourself? Do you withdraw, feel sad or cry? How long does it take you to get over feeling rejected?

_____

_____

_____

If a friend asked you for advice on what he or she should do if having a difficult time gaining the friendship or acceptance of someone, what would you tell your friend?

_____

_____

What do you try to cover up about yourself? What are you most afraid that others will not like about you? Why do you think they won't like that part of you?

_____

_____

Sometimes I am meeting a part of myself for the first time.

—Jennifer Leigh

What do you think Jennifer's quote means?

_____

_____

The Real Me . . . Do You Know Me the Real Me?

Quiet and Shy—Not!

I know there are times when my parents and teachers—even some of my friends—see me differently than I really am. They think I'm quiet and shy, really smart but not very cool. What they don't know is that's who I am when I am with them, but it's not who I really am. The real me comes out when I'm around guys who are more like me—like Tom Henderson and Graham Barry. Tom and Graham bring out the best in me, the real me. We met each other on the first day of the Young Scientist contest last year. Even though the three of us don't get a chance to see each other very often, we're still the best of friends. Tom and Graham know me better than any of the kids at school know me. The three of us just clicked. We really understand each other. I have more fun with them than anyone else. I always feel happy and in a good mood, even when I'm working through a problem, when I talk with Tom and Graham. With them, I'm my "real shade."
—Chad Dalton, 16

Who understands you—the real you—better than anybody else? How do you know this? Why is it this person is able to understand you? Is it because he or she is just like you, or for some other reason? How long have you known this person? Do you think you will be friends all of your lives?

_____

_____

_____

Describe a time you felt sure someone "really knew you," and then something happened that made you realize that person didn't know you as well as you thought. For example, did someone ever mistrust you or doubt your word? What happened? What was the incident that showed you this person didn't know the real you? Who was the person? How did you feel about what happened? How did you feel toward the other person?

_____

_____

How did the incident change the relationship between the two of you? Did it strain the friendship, or make it stronger? Are you still friends or did you part company? What did the incident teach you?

_____

_____

If Only You Knew . . . I'd Like You to Know . . .

Sometimes we need to help our friends get to know "the real me." What two things do you wish all of your friends knew about you? Why *don't* they know? How can you let them know?

I wish all my friends knew:

_____

_____

I can let them know by:

_____

_____

When you're a teen,
you get pulled in a lot of different
directions, especially when you're
trying to meet the expectations of
different
people—all of whom are important
to you.

—Jennifer Leigh

Name the two people whose expectations of you matter the most to you. Next to the person's name, describe what it is he or she expects of you, as well as how you feel about meeting those expectations.

EXAMPLE:

<u>Who</u>: My best friend.

<u>Expectation:</u> My best friend expects me to be her friend, even when she does things I don't like, such as always expecting me to let her copy my homework.

<u>How I feel about meeting this expectation:</u> I feel uncomfortable when I have to just go along with things I don't feel right about.

1) <u>Who:</u> _____

<u>Expectation:</u> _____
_____

<u>How I feel about meeting this expectation:</u> _____
_____

2) <u>Who:</u> _____

<u>Expectation:</u> _____

_____

<u>How I feel about meeting this expectation:</u> _____

_____

Decisions: Meeting Others Halfway

You and your good friend have made plans to do something together—just the two of you. Then at the last minute your friend calls you and explains that a "special someone" phoned and wants that person to "come along."

Would you:

1. Tell your friend to phone his or her "special someone" and explain that the evening has been set up with just the two of you and the two of them should make plans for a different evening?

2. Tell your friend that the two of you can reschedule your plans for spending the evening together at another time;

3. Say, "Fine," even though you feel differently; or, find a way to meet each other halfway—to compromise?

4. _____

_____

Are you good at compromising? Or, do you find you always give in and allow the other person to do what he or she would like, even if it means your needs aren't met. Or, do you insist on having your way, sometimes even at the expense of the other person's needs?

_____

_____

Describe a time when you had to meet someone halfway. What was going on? What were you being asked to do? Who was involved? What happened?

_____

_____

How did things turn out? Did everyone "win"? Did everyone get his or her needs met? How do you know?

_____

_____

How did you feel about the outcome? How did
the other person feel about the outcome? How did
having everyone get his or her needs met contribute
to your positive feelings of self?

_____

_____

Your family is having relatives over for your little
brother's birthday, and you've been asked to attend
a really special party for a good friend. What
compromise would you propose to your parents?
Explain how your willingness to meet others
halfway was good for everyone involved.

_____

_____

_____

Do you find it easier to meet some friends—more
so than others—halfway? Why do you think this is
so?

_____

_____

The most important trip you take in life is meeting others halfway.

—Henry Boyle

Standing Up For Yourself

Sometimes, there's a fine line between going along, doing the things others want you to do, and being true to yourself —listening to your own voice and preferences, acting on what you believe, and doing what's important and best for you.

What does this quote mean to you?

_____

_____

Where do you draw the line between doing what others want and being true to yourself? Write about a time you were "true to your own color"—the self you know better than anyone else does—though you knew that someone special wouldn't think you were cool for making the choice you did. What was the situation? What was going on? Why weren't you and the other person in agreement? How did you stick up for yourself?

_____

_____

_____

_____

Self-Worth: What You Think of You

Self-worth —what we think about ourselves—shows up in the things we say and do. We may even misinterpret the words and actions of others because of the view we hold of ourselves.

What does this quote mean to you?

_____

_____

What is a "Friend"?

A good friend is someone who understands us, someone we can count on, someone who helps us through tough times, someone we can be ourselves with and have fun with. That's why friends are *friends*.

How would you define a *good* friend?

_____

_____

_____

What are the three most important qualities you look for in a friend?

1. _____

2. _____

3. _____

The Importance of Friends

Why is it important <u>to you</u> to have friends?

_____

_____

How is having "friends" different from having a "best friend"?

_____

_____

The Difference Between a Friend and a _Best_ Friend

A best friend becomes the "best" friend because that person makes it okay to be yourself.

What does this quote mean to you?

_____

_____

Who is your very best friend? How long has this person been your "best" friend? Describe your *best friend*.

_____

_____

Why is that person's friendship important to you? How does that person make it "safe to be yourself"? What is the most personal secret you've shared with your best friend?

_____

_____

Do you think this person will be your best friend for always, or just for now?

_____

_____

My Best Friend's Best Traits

What is it about your best friend that you like the most? List three traits about that person that makes him or her special to you.

1. _____

_____

2. _____

_____

3. _____

_____

*A good friend listens.
And hears you.*
—**Jenna Reynolds, 15**

Who Considers You a "Best Friend"?

Who considers you his or her best friend? How do you know this? Why do you think the friendship the two of you share is important to your friend?

_____

_____

_____

What two things do you think your friend would list as YOUR best friendship qualities?

1. _____

_____

2. _____

_____

You will be my friend—forever.
—**Chelsea Sudberry, 17**

Breakups . . . Makeups

Write about a time you had a major disagreement with your best friend. When did it occur? What caused the argument? Was anyone else involved? Was anyone "in the wrong"?

_____

_____

How were you able to resolve your differences? Who made the first move to repair the friendship— you or your friend?

_____

_____

Did the "makeup" include an explanation as to what went wrong, or was it simply an "I'm sorry" but the two of you didn't really talk out why there were hurt feelings in the first place? Exactly what did the other person—or you—say or do to make up?

_____

_____

Actions: Working Through Disagreements

How did being at odds with your friend make you feel? How were you affected by the breakup? For example, did you go about your life certain that everything would work out in the end? Did you give your friend a little space and not get too worked up over it? Or were you so upset that you couldn't sleep, were irritable and neglected your responsibilities— such as homework and chores? Or did you write, phone or talk with him or her to try to resolve the matter as soon as possible?

_____

_____

Sometimes a disagreement is seemingly petty and after it's over, we wonder why we made such a big deal of it in the first place. And sometimes a disagreement can be a good way to "clear the air," to talk about an issue that the two of you need to discuss. Think back over a recent upset. What did it teach you about yourself? What did it teach you about the other person? What were you surprised to learn?

I discovered that: _____

_____

I was surprised that: _____

_____

_____

Do You Have More than One Best Friend?

Do you have more than one best friend? How many best friends do you have?

_____

Does your best friend mind that you have other close friends? How do you know?

_____

_____

In what ways are your friends also friends with each other? For example, do they play on the same sport teams or go to the same school? Are they friends because one of the things they have in common is a friendship with you?

_____

_____

_____

How Are Your Friends Alike?

In what two ways are your two closest friends alike?

❤ _____

❤ _____

In what two ways are those same two friends different?

❤ _____

❤ _____

How does having friends who are different from each other make your life more interesting?

_____

_____

Friends: Two's Company, is Three a Crowd?

Write about a time when a friend made it clear that he or she was to be your only friend—period! Who was that friend? How did he or she let you know this? Describe the incident or circumstances that brought this about. How did you feel about it, and what did you do? Are you still friends?

_____

_____

_____

_____

Roma Kipling, 17, who you read about earlier in Chapter Two, said her grandmother was very special to her. Do you have an adult friend as close and loving as "Grams"? Who?

_____

Can your parents, grandparents, or even brothers or sisters be a "close" friend? Why do you feel this way?

_____

_____

Friends: Helping You Cope with Tough Times

Describe an incident when a friend helped you cope with a really tough time. What were you going through? Who was the friend? In what ways did your friend help you get through this time?

_____

_____

Did the support you got from your friend surprise you, or did you expect that he or she would respond in this way?

_____

_____

How did the way your friend responded to you during this tough time change the relationship you share? For example, did it strengthen your bond (or did it tear you apart); do you talk more frequently now; do you trust each other implicitly; or, know where each other is "coming from"?

_____

_____

_____

Friends and Secrets

A good friend is someone with whom we can have fun and share our innermost thoughts lofty and noble goals, secrets, and our hopes, joys and fears.

Have you ever shared a secret with your best friend? Did your friend also share a secret, or just you? How long had this person been your friend before you shared your secret?

_____

_____

How many secrets do you and your best friend have between you? What is the best secret you have ever shared with a good friend?

_____

_____

Have you ever had a friend promise to keep a secret and then break that promise? Why did your friend break the trust? What happened as a result?

_____

_____

Did you and your friend ever forgive each other? Exactly what was said between the two of you? Is that person still your friend? How do you feel about that person now?

_____

_____

Have you ever betrayed someone's trust in you to keep a promise? What was the promise? Why did you break the trust? What happened? Who found out? What happened then?

_____

_____

_____

How did you feel about yourself for breaking the trust? How did doing this change the friendship?

_____

_____

_____

What secret is so big you never told anyone, not even your best friend? Why haven't you told anyone?

_____

_____

Actions: Listening

A good friend is someone who allows you a safe space to share your thoughts and goals without worry of being judged, criticized or made to feel silly.

What does this quote mean to you?

_____

_____

Earlier in this book you read a poem called, "Our Friendship is Real" by Peggy Nunziata, who in a poem wrote:

I've seen lots of people come and go,
Saying and doing whatever—careless, you know?
That's why your friendship means so much to me,
When I'm with you, I feel secure, whole, and free.

What is a "real" friendship? How can you tell if a friendship is "real"?

_____

_____

Describe an incident that tested your friendship— one that showed you *if* your friend was *really* your friend. What happened? Who was involved? How did you feel about what was going on? How did things turn out in the end? Are you still friends?

_____

_____

_____

_____

Being a "Real" Friend

Do you think it's possible for someone to be a "real" friend without being a close friend? Whom do you consider a "real" friend, even though you aren't close friends, and why?

_____

_____

    List two "real" friends you can count on and describe what it is each one does to let you know you can trust him or her to be there for you.

A Real Friend: _____

How I know this person is my friend: _____

_____

_____

A Real Friend: _____

How I know this person is my friend: _____

_____

_____

What one person more than anyone else taught you the most important lesson about being a good friend? What was the lesson? Why was it so meaningful to you? What did you learn from this lesson? How do you feel about the person who taught this lesson?

_____

_____

_____

The Rules for Being MY Friend

In Chapter Two, Elmer Adrian wrote a poem called "Did I Pass Your Test for Friends?" What are the rules for being *your* friend? For example, do you expect your friends to stick up for you even when you are in the wrong? Do you expect a good friend to compliment you when you do something especially good, like ace an exam? What are three of the most basic "rules" you expect someone to "pass" in order to be your friend?

Rule #1: _____

_____

Rule #2: _____

_____

Rule #3: _____

_____

Do your friends have rules for being their friend? Do you feel they are pretty much like your "rules," or are they very different?

_____

_____

List two of the rules your best friend has for the friendship the two of you share.

Rule #1: _____

_____

Rule #2: _____

_____

How do you know these rules are understood? For example, did you and your friend talk about them, or are they unwritten rules that are understood?

_____

_____

When was the last time one of these rules was clarified? How was that done—was it discussed, or did someone get upset with you because you violated the expected "code of conduct"?

_____

_____

_____

Ending Friendships

Is it possible to be friends with everyone, or do you think that some people make better friends than do others? How do you know when a friend is right for you, while another is not?

_____

_____

Did you ever have a friend who was a bad influence on you? Who was this person? How could you tell—in what ways was this person a bad influence? Is this person still your friend?

_____

_____

When someone is not right for you, not "good" for you, how do you say "no go" to the friendship? Do you just ignore the person and hope he or she will get the message and stop hanging around you, or do you tell the person directly (or ask your friends to tell the person)?

_____

_____

_____

In Chapter Two, Belinda Carr wrote a story called, "Sometimes You Just Outgrow Your Friends." Have you ever outgrown a friend? How did you know?

_____

_____

Write about a time you had to end a friendship. Who was the friend you had to "give up"? How did you know you needed to let the friendship go? How did the person feel about things?

_____

_____

_____

Making Friends: New Faces, New Places

Is it easy for you to make new friends? How do you know if someone else wants to be your friend? What are the signs?

_____

_____

_____

How can you tell if that person will be right for you as a friend? Can you tell right away, or is it something that comes with time?

_____

_____

What is the best way to be a friend to someone new, someone you don't know very well?

_____

_____

How would you handle it if you really wanted to be friends with someone, but you thought your other friends would disapprove?

_____

_____

Is there someone with whom you would like to become better friends? Who is it? What is it about this person that makes you want to be his or her friend?

_____

_____

List two things you intend to do to get to know this person better.

EXAMPLE:

I would ask him or her if he or she wants to sit with me and some of my friends at the school assembly.

1. _____

   _____

2. _____

   _____

A Friend Helps Me Grow into Myself

*Friends help us grow into who
we already are.*

—Jennifer Leigh

What does it mean to "grow into who we already are"?

_____

_____

One of the wonderful things about good friends is that they help us see the good in ourselves. This reaffirms that we are doing the right things, that we are a person who is trying to make the best of our lives and getting through the rough spots in positive ways. In what ways do your friends help you "grow into who you are?"

_____

_____

Being My Own Best Friend

Sometimes we don't think about friendship as an important relationship that we have with ourselves as well as with others. Yet it's important that we be a good friend to ourselves. List three ways you are a friend to yourself?

1. _____

2. _____

3. _____

What two requests would it make? In what ways would you like to treat yourself even better?

EXAMPLE:

<u>Dear Self, Please eat breakfast. I get so tired before lunch when you don't.</u>

Dear Self: _____

_____

Dear Self: _____

_____

Being My Own Friend

Being a good friend to yourself makes you a good friend to others. List three ways in which being a good friend to yourself makes you a better friend to others.

EXAMPLE:

<u>It makes me feel good about myself so I have a more
positive outlook to share with my friends.</u>

1. _____

   _____

2. _____

   _____

3. _____

   _____

Always remember you are your own best friend.
Friends may come and go but *you* will be there to
face yourself. You will be there for yourself with
the consequences of your choices—good and bad.
You will be alone with *you*. So treat yourself with
respect and the love you deserve!

How Your Brain Decides If You Will Become Addicted—Or Not

Information and Encouragement for Teens, with Stories by Teens and Young Adults
Jennifer Leigh Youngs, A.A. | Bettie B. Youngs, Ph.D., Ed.D.

- *"using," dependency and addiction*
- *if you or a friend can't stop using*
- *Withdrawal, Relapse, and Recovery*
- *cool ways to say "no"*

Book: 978-1-940784-99-1
e-book: 978-1-940784-98-4

Setting and Achieving Goals that Matter to ME

Information and Encouragement for Teens, with Stories by Teens
Jennifer Leigh Youngs, A.A. | Bettie B. Youngs, Ph.D., Ed.D.

- *discovering what's important TO ME*
- *hobbies, talents, interests, apptitudes*
- *hopes, aspirations and dreaming big*
- *my goal-setting workbook*

Book: 978-1-940784-97-7
e-book: 978-1-940784-96-0

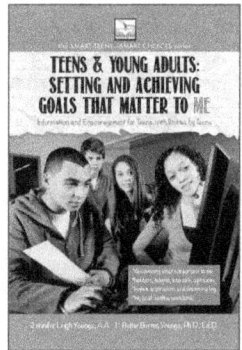

Managing Stress, Pressure, and the Ups and Downs of Life

Information, Encouragement and Inspiration—with commentary by teens
Jennifer Leigh Youngs, A.A. | Bettie B. Youngs, Ph.D., Ed.D.

- *great ways to manage stress and pressure*
- *how stress works for—and against—you*
- *physical, emotional and behavioral signs of stress*
- *staying cool under pressure*

Book: 978-1-940784-80-9
e-book: 978-1-940784-81-6

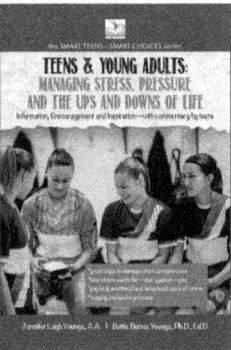

The 10 Commandments and the Secret Each One Guards—For You

Information and Inspirational Short Stories
Bettie B. Youngs, Ph.D., Ed.D. | Jennifer Leigh Youngs, A.A.

- *how the Commandments speak to you*
- *the secret each Commandment guards*
- *using your faith to guide the choices you make*
- *how to be confident and bold in your faith*

Book: 978-1-940784-95-3
e-book: 978-1-940784-94-6

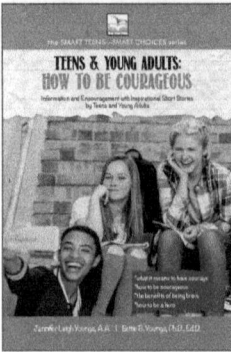

How to Be Courageous

Encouragment and Inspirational Short Stories by Teens and Young Adults
Jennifer Leigh Youngs, A.A. | Bettie B. Youngs, Ph.D., Ed.D.

- *the importance of being courageous*
- *the benefits of being brave*
- *how to be a hero*

Book: 978-1-940784-93-9
e-book: 978-1-940784-92-2

Growing Your Confidence and Self-Esteem

Information, Encouragement and Inspirational Short Stories by Teens and Young Adults
Jennifer Leigh Youngs, A.A. | Bettie B. Youngs, Ph.D., Ed.D.

- *being on good terms with YOU*
- *feeling "good enough"*
- *the power of confience*
- *liking the face in the mirror*
- *being happy and "forward looking"*

Book: 978-1-940784-86-1
e-book: 978-1-940784-87-8

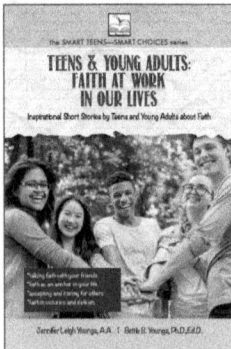

Faith at Work in Our Lives

Information, Encouragement and Inspirational Short Stories by Teens and Young Adults
Jennifer Leigh Youngs, A.A. | Bettie B. Youngs, Ph.D., Ed.D.

- *talking faith with your friends*
- *faith as an anchor in your life*
- *accepting and caring for others*
- *faith in victories and defeats*

Book: 978-1-940784-78-6
e-book: 978-1-940784-79-3

Understanding Feelings of Love

Inspirational Short Stories by Teens and Young Adults
Jennifer Leigh Youngs, A.A. | Bettie B. Youngs, Ph.D., Ed.D.

- *the lessons of love*
- *setting boundaries important to you*
- *4 ways to be a great boy/girlfriend*
- *when love relationships end*

Book: 978-1-940784-75-5
e-book: 978-1-940784-74-8

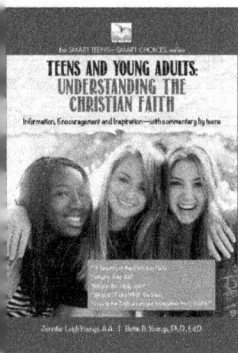

Understanding the Christian Faith

Information, Encouragement and Inspirational Short Stories by Teens and Young Adults
Jennifer Leigh Youngs, A.A. | Bettie B. Youngs, Ph.D., Ed.D.

- *9 Tenants of the Christian Faith*
- *What is Free Will*
- *What is the Holly Spirit*
- *What is "Reap What You Sow"*
- *How is the Bible as unique from other Holy Books?*

Book: 978-1-940784-76-2
e-book: 978-1-940784-77-9

How to be a Good Friend

Information and Encouragement with Inspirational Short Stories
by Teens and Young Adults
Jennifer Leigh Youngs, A.A. | Bettie B. Youngs, Ph.D., Ed.D.

- *understanding friendships*
- *how to be a good friend*
- *making, keeping, and ending friendships*
- *mending hurt feelings*

Book: 978-1-940784-73-1
e-book: 978-1-940784-72-4

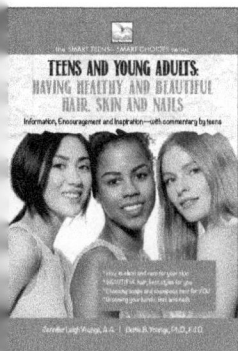

Having Healthy and Beautiful Hair, Skin and Nails

Information, Encouragement and Inspiration—with commentary by teens
Jennifer Leigh Youngs, A.A. | Bettie B. Youngs, Ph.D., Ed.D.

- *how to clean and care for your skin*
- *BEAUTIFUL hair; best styles for you*
- *choosing soaps and shampoos best for YOU*
- *grooming your hands, feet, and nails*

Book: 978-1-940784-84-7
e-book: 978-1-940784-85-4

The Power of Being Kind, Courteous and Thoughtful

Information, Encouragement and Inspirational Short Stories by Teens and Young Adults
Jennifer Leigh Youngs, A.A. | Bettie B. Youngs, Ph.D., Ed.D.

- *the power of being KIND*
- *the importance of being COURTEOUS*
- *how to be "THOUGHTFUL"*

Book: 978-1-940784-82-3
e-book: 978-1-940784-83-0

www.ingramcontent.com/pod-product-compliance
Lightning Source LLC
Chambersburg PA
CBHW031519270326
41930CB00006B/436